An American Bird Conservancy
Compact Guide

Paul Lehman
Ornithological Editor

The **American Bird Conservancy (ABC)** is a U.S.-based, not-for-profit organization formed to unify bird conservation efforts across the Americas and dedicated to the conservation of birds throughout the Western Hemisphere. ABC practices conservation through partnership, bringing together the partners whose expertise and resources are best suited to each task.

The **ABC Policy Council** has a membership of more than 70 organizations sharing a common interest in the conservation of birds. Composed of ornithologists, policy specialists, educators, and general bird enthusiasts, the Council is a professional forum for exchanging information and discussing critical and emerging bird conservation issues. The Council provides policy and scientific advice to conservationists, stimulates a network of support for conservation policies through national, state, and local groups, and directly accomplishes conservation through ABC.

ABC is a working member of **Partners in Flight (PIF)**, an Americas-wide coalition of more than 150 organizations and government agencies dedicated to bird conservation. Initially begun to find ways to reverse the decline in neotropical migratory bird species, PIF has broadened its scope to include all non-game birds in the Americas. PIF links birders, hunters, government, industry, landowners, and other citizens in a unified effort to conserve bird populations and habitats.

Many North American "birds" found in this guide spend more than half their lives in Latin America and the Caribbean. The needs for bird conservation in this region are at least as great as in the U.S. Through PIF, ABC is building U.S. support for capable, but often underfunded, conservation partners throughout the Americas.

PIF's bird conservation strategy, called the **Flight Plan**, can be obtained from ABC, the National Fish and Wildlife Foundation, or the U.S. Fish and Wildlife Service. PIF's National Coordinator serves on ABC's staff, and ABC helps implement the Flight Plan through its Important Bird Areas (IBA) initiative. ABC members receive *Bird Conservation*, the magazine about PIF and American bird conservation.

ALL THE
BIRDS
OF PREY

BY JACK L. GRIGGS

red-shouldered hawk

HarperPerennial
A Division of HarperCollins*Publishers*

Designed by Jack L. Griggs & Peg Alrich

Edited by Virginia Croft

Additional ornithological editing
by Jerry Ligouri

Illustrations reformatted by John E. Griggs
from the original illustrations by Hans Peeters
published in
All the Birds of North America

ALL THE BIRDS OF PREY. Copyright © 1999 by Jack L. Griggs. All rights
reserved. Printed in Hong Kong. No part of this book may be used or
reproduced in any manner whatsoever without written permission except
in the case of brief quotations embodied in critical articles and reviews.
For information address HarperCollins Publishers, Inc., 10 East 53rd
Street, New York, NY 10022.

HarperCollins books may be purchased for educational, business, or
sales promotional use. For information please write: Special Markets
Department, HarperCollins Publishers, Inc., 10 East 53rd Street, New
York, NY 10022.

FIRST EDITION

Library of Congress Cataloging-in-Publication Data
    Griggs, Jack L.
      All the birds of prey / Jack L. Griggs
          p.   cm.
      Includes index.
      ISBN 0-06-273654-X
    1. Birds of prey—North America—Identification. I. Title.
QL696.F3G748 1999
598.9'097—dc21   98-41934
                                                      CIP

99 00 01 02 ❖/RRD 10 9 8 7 6 5 4 3 2 1

CONTENTS

HAWKWATCH SITES
a foreword by Jerry Ligouri

IDENTIFYING BIRDS OF PREY

CHECKLIST AND INDEX

HAWK-WATCH SITES

by
JERRY LIGUORI

Hawks follow certain paths in migration. They are capable of powering themselves along a broad front in direct, sustained flight, but they take routes that let them conserve energy. Whether in spring, when migrants wing north to their nesting grounds, or in fall, as they return south, their routes are fixed by weather and the lay of the land.

Some mountain ridges are famous for attracting migrating hawks. As wind strikes a ridge, an updraft is produced that provides hawks with a cushion of air for easy flight. Often raptors will ride updrafts for many miles without a single beat of their wings. A succession of ridges and favorable winds can provide a migrating hawk with an almost effortless journey.

Water barriers concentrate large numbers of raptors. Most hawks faced with crossing an extensive body of water choose to follow the shoreline instead. The northwestern shore of Lake Superior, for example, interrupts southbound hawks along a broad front and leads them all to Hawk Ridge in Duluth, MN, at the southwestern tip of the shoreline.

Raptors include all the birds of prey except owls. In this text, *hawk* and *raptor* are used interchangeably.

One reason hawks prefer flying over land is the presence of thermals—pockets of warm rising air. Hawks gain altitude effortlessly in a thermal and can then glide on fixed wings for a long period. Thermals are produced by heat

Many hawks will often ascend in the same thermal. The group is termed a "kettle" for its similarity to a pot of simmering water with bubbles rising to the top.

radiating from the earth. Rocky surfaces radiate more heat than surrounding vegetation, creating a rising column of warm air. Most hawks don't take to the sky in the morning until the earth's surface is warmed by the sun.

Hawks concentrate along the Atlantic and Pacific coasts during migration. Peninsulas funnel them to points where they may be seen in large numbers. On the Pacific coast, southbound migrants are tallied in the greatest numbers at the Golden Gate National Recreation Area on the peninsula just north of San Francisco. On the Atlantic coast, Cape May Point, NJ (by Delaware Bay), and Cape Charles, VA (by Chesapeake Bay), trap southbound migrants, which must either cross or go around large bays.

THE 16 RAPTORS THAT MIGRATE THROUGH THE EAST

bald eagle
golden eagle
peregrine falcon
goshawk
harrier
broad-winged hawk
Cooper's hawk
red-tailed hawk
red-shouldered hawk
rough-legged hawk
sharp-shinned hawk
kestrel
merlin
osprey
black vulture
turkey vulture

The exact timing of migration depends upon the species and the weather. Generally, hawks avoid a weather front. They may be forced along the edge of a front or build up behind a slow-moving front. Each hawkwatch has its own optimum weather conditions and time for watching migrating hawks.

The most renowned hawkwatch site of all is Hawk Mountain in Kempton, PA. Once a place where shooters lined the ridges for live target practice, it became Hawk Mountain Sanctuary in the autumn of 1934 and conducted its first

**SOME ADDITIONAL
FALL APPALACHIAN
HAWKWATCH SITES**

Mount Wachusett
near Princeton, MA

Franklin Mountain
near Oneonta, NY

Hook Mountain
near Nyack, NY

Raccoon Ridge
near Blairstown, NJ

Montclair, NJ
(spring site as well)

Militia Hill
near Philadelphia, PA
(a relatively new site,
hosts more broad-
wings than established
Appalachian sites and
tallies large numbers
of bald eagles)

Harvey's Knob
near Buchanan, VA

**Wind directions are
called by their ori-
gins. Thus, a north-
westerly wind blows
from the northwest
to the southeast.**

official hawk count. By 1997, the Hawk Migration Association of North America was cataloging data from 1,066 sites across the United States and Canada. Every year new hawk migration sites are discovered and new hawk-watchers join experienced enthusiasts to enjoy the spectacle. Wherever you are in the United States or southern Canada, there is a hawkwatch site nearby or one that is waiting to be discovered.

The Appalachian Mountains provide a continuous range of ridges that includes some of the best hawkwatch sites in the East, notably the venerable Hawk Mountain. With its beautiful overlook and spectacular, often head-on views of raptors, Hawk Mountain is a truly special site. Watchers wait in great anticipation for the fall broad-winged hawk migration, which usually peaks between September 15 and 21. Northwesterly winds after a cold front during this period may produce broad-wings by the thousands. Flights of sharp-shins, kestrels, and ospreys also peak with the broad-wings.

A month later, toward the third week of October, the excitement at Hawk Mountain escalates again as visitors anticipate the push of goshawks, red-tailed hawks, red-shouldered hawks, and eagles. The golden eagle is an especially sought-after species on the mountain, and from the north lookout, eye-level views are not uncommon. Sensational hawk flights carry on through the first half of November, including daily flights of up to a dozen goshawks.

Along the Atlantic coast, the most visited hawk-watch site is Cape May Point, NJ. Dominant westerly winds throughout autumn push massive numbers of migrating birds toward the Atlantic coast on their way south. Accipiters, harriers, and ospreys are seen in record numbers at Cape May Point, but what draws most interest is the outstanding falcon flights. Kestrels, merlins, and peregrines (all falcons) are observed in greater numbers here than at any other site in North America. Over 500 merlins have been seen in a single day.

Falcon migration peaks at Cape May Point from the last week of September to the first week of October, but there are consistent hawk flights from September through November. Northwesterly winds usually produce the largest single-day counts, although peregrine falcons often peak during southeasterly winds. On days with light northwesterly winds, hawks soar at high altitudes on thermals, whereas during strong northwesterly winds they travel singly at low altitudes. The various postures and silhouettes exhibited as they pass high and low challenge even the experienced observers' skills.

Along the Great Lakes in fall, Hawk Ridge in Duluth, MN, attracts greater numbers of bald eagles and goshawks than anywhere else in the world. It also hosts amazing flights of many other raptors, including rough-legged hawks and golden eagles. Multiple sightings of the rare dark form of the broad-winged hawk are recorded each fall as well. Counts recently begun each spring at Hawk Ridge have revealed a considerable migration of bald eagles.

Hawk Ridge is located atop a ridge overlooking the shoreline of Lake Superior. The view of the shoreline and of the migrating hawks is spectacular. Raptors that are forced southwest along the northern shore of Lake Superior are attracted to the updrafts provided by Hawk Ridge at the southwestern tip of the lake. The flight line of the birds provides astounding views of both the uppersides and undersides of migrant hawks. Westerly to northerly winds are required to concentrate massive numbers of hawks along the shoreline, with northwest being the most conducive wind direction.

The timetable for fall hawk migration at Hawk Ridge is consistent with that for Hawk Mountain and most sites in the United States.

In spring along the Great Lakes, two hawk-watch sites on the southern shore of Lake Ontario experience the most diverse spring

SOME ADDITIONAL GREAT LAKES HAWK-WATCH SITES

Marathon, Ontario
north shore of Lake Superior
(fall)

Beamer Conservation Area
near Grimsby, Ontario
(spring)

Enger Tower
in Duluth, MN
(the spring sister site to Hawk Ridge, established in 1997)

Hawk Cliffs
near Port Stanley, Ontario
(fall)

Holiday Beach, Ontario, north shore of Lake Erie just east of Detroit, close to Lake Erie Metropark
(fall)

Lake Erie Metropark
south of Detroit, MI
(fall, some of the largest flights of any US site but many are high-flying specks)

raptor migration in the US. Hawks can be observed along the entire southern shoreline from mid-February to early June as they head east around Lake Ontario, but two points about 100 miles apart are where flights concentrate—Braddock Bay in Greece, NY, and Derby Hill in Mexico, NY, at the southeast corner of Lake Ontario. The sites record equal numbers of migrants over a season, but they experience quite different daily flights.

Strong southwesterly winds produce big flights at Braddock Bay; strong southeast winds work best at Derby Hill. Located atop an 80-foot high bluff, Derby Hill provides an eye-level view of some migrants, whereas many birds tend to appear as specks over Braddock Bay.

Regardless, both sites have had world-record-high daily flights for harriers, red-shouldered hawks, and red-tailed hawks. Outstanding counts of many other raptors, including bald eagles, are tallied as well. Late March to early April is the peak migration time, but harriers, accipiters, and kestrels peak toward mid-April. Ospreys and broad-wings are most numerous toward the end of April and in early May. In the fall, an incredible flight of young red-tails occurs from early August to early September.

In spring, hawks also collect on the southern shore of Lake Superior, where they follow the shoreline east until reaching a small peninsula called Whitefish Point in Michigan. Faced with Lake Superior to the north and Whitefish Bay to the east, raptors concentrate before embarking across the bay. Late April through May brings excellent flights of sharp-shins and broad-wings, which tend to fly in large groups, or kettles, before leaving the point.

It is the record-high daily and seasonal counts of rough-legged hawks that primarily distinguish Whitefish Point. Rough-legs are strong-flying, long-winged buteos and will attempt water crossings more readily than most other buteos. Because of the spring snow cover, which reflects sunlight and illuminates plumage details on the undersides of the birds, which would normally be invisible, observers are provided with stellar views of the countless plumage variations rough-legs exhibit.

Western hawkwatches provide a different experience than eastern ones. Broad-winged hawks and red-shouldered hawks, which are numerous in the East, are rare in the West, whereas the opposite is true for species such as Swainson's and ferruginous hawks and prairie falcons. Most western hawkwatch sites also record more golden eagles and sub-species such as Harlan's red-tailed hawk and the pale prairie merlin. Cooper's hawks are nearly as numerous as sharp-shins at some western sites. In the East, ten sharp-shins will pass, on average, for every Cooper's.

Along the Pacific coast, the Golden Gate hawkwatch just north of San Francisco is the most popular site and tallies the greatest numbers of raptors. As at most coastal sites, falcons are recorded in good numbers at Golden Gate, peaking in mid-September to early October. The powerful falcons are little influenced by wind and can be observed under most weather conditions. The coastline provides them with an excellent opportunity for a meal on the go—a duck, shorebird, or migrating songbird.

While broad-winged hawks are rare in the West, one of the attractions of Golden Gate is regular tallies of rare dark-form broad-winged hawks. The many color variations of the red-tailed hawk can be observed here also.

The Goshute Mountains near Wendover, UT, at the western edge of the Great Salt Lake desert, is the site of the most significant autumn western raptor migration. Discovered in 1979, the Goshutes hawkwatch offers unobstructed 360-degree views of migrating hawks so ideal that binoculars are at times unnecessary. Flights peak in mid-September, when a good day may produce more than 100 each of red-tails, sharp-shins, Cooper's hawks, and kestrels.

A half-dozen golden eagles may also sail by along with Swainson's hawks, goshawks, and prairie falcons. Westerly winds usually produce the biggest daily flights. Migration continues into November, when heavy snowfall usually causes the Goshutes site to be abandoned.

In the Southwest, at the Cibola National Forest near Albuquerque, NM, the Sandia hawkwatch hosts a phenomenal flight of raptors in spring. March brings a big push of golden eagles. Red-tailed hawks and prairie falcons peak in early April, with accipiters and kestrels peaking soon after. Few sites tally more prairie falcons than Sandia. The zone-tailed hawk, a scarce migrant restricted to the Southwest, is seen annually.

The Sandia site is located on an outcropping of bare watermelon-colored rocks. Significant flights occur with light winds or strong westerly winds. An immense updraft is produced as strong northwesterly winds strike the steep face of an adjacent ridge east of the watch. Hawks ride the updraft like an elevator straight up toward the top of the ridge. Observers willing to climb to the top of the east ridge come face to face with the raptors.

On the Gulf of Mexico, Hazel Bazemore County Park, near the shoreline in Corpus Christi, TX, is the premier broad-winged hawk site in the US. Broad-wings collect along the

SOME ADDITIONAL GULF COAST HAWKWATCH SITES

Smith Point
east of Houston, TX
(fall)

Bentsen-Rio Grande Valley State Park, TX
(spring and fall)

Santa Ana NWR, TX
(spring and fall)

South Padre Island, TX
(spring and fall, peregrine falcons a specialty)

Veracruz, Mexico
(fall, millions of migrants recorded each season)

shore of the Gulf of Mexico in migration, and nearly a million raptors, most of them broad-wings, are recorded in spring and fall at Hazel Bazemore. Swainson's hawks and Mississippi kites, among others, are also seen in good numbers. In North America, only Veracruz, Mexico, records more migrating raptors.

Most of the raptors at Hazel Bazemore fly high. Massive swarms of hawks rise in a good thermal, while those at the top exit and glide in squadrons toward the next thermal, where they regain the altitude lost gliding. Spring migration peaks from late March to late April; fall numbers crest from late September through early October. Westerly winds are usually the most productive, but large flights can occur on any day that produces good thermals.

More hawkwatch sites deserve description than space permits. There is much to be learned at all of them. Most are manned and operated by professional organizations that make special efforts to hire biologists and educators to record accurate data and tend to the public's needs. Workshops are offered at several sites, and hawk-counters and interns often help visitors identify birds. It is also possible at all sites to simply enjoy great views of one magnificent hawk after another without ever naming a single bird.

At many hawkwatches, not only are hawks counted, but some are briefly captured in fine nets and banded. Naturalists conduct banding demonstrations for the public at some of the most prominent sites.

HOW TO LOOK AT BIRDS OF PREY

RED-TAILED HAWK

Female hawks and owls of nearly all species are larger than males, often noticeably so.

Given a good view, either perched or in flight, a hawk or an owl is easily distinguished from other birds. Their adaptations for hunting prey are distinctive and similar to others of their kind whether they are massive birds, like the golden eagle and great horned owl, or weigh only a few ounces, like the kestrel and elf owl.

Both hawks and owls have strong toes (talons) for catching prey and large, hooked upper bills for dismembering it. Most hawks also have bare skin above the bill (the cere) and a protective bony ridge over the eyes that contributes to their characteristic fierce appearance. Owls are distinguished by their large heads and the large discs surrounding their eyes—areas that help direct sound to the sensitive hearing apparatus that makes up a large portion of the head. Both hawks and owls tend to perch distinctively upright.

In flight, hawks display large wings with characteristically powerful wing beats—when they choose to fly under their own power. One of their most distinguishing traits is their preference for soaring in thermals or updrafts without flapping or only occasionally flapping. They share their mastery of the air with other birds that hunt from the wing, such as gulls. A distant soaring gull can be distinguished from a hawk by its shape and shallow, easy wing beat. A gull's wings are pointed and droop downward, and its head projects in front of its wing about the same distance as its tail extends behind. Most hawks have broader, squarer-tipped wings, and all have smaller heads and longer tails than gulls.

Shape and flight style are important marks used to distinguish hawks in flight from one another. Note the frequency of the wing beat and its character—deep or shallow, stiff or fluid. When judging shape, look at the relative projection of the head and tail and the outline of the wing. Hawks can hold their wings in different sets, creating many different apparent shapes, but in a full soar or in powered flight, the subtle differences in wing shape between species can be studied.

HAND

WRIST

SECONDARIES

PRIMARIES

SWAINSON'S HAWK

Most names used to describe parts of a bird of prey are fairly predictable—back, crown, bill, etc. Hand and wrist are often used to describe portions of the wing. Secondaries and primaries refer to the inner and outer flight feathers, respectively.

A wing might be plank-like, as in the bald eagle, with straight leading and trailing edges and a fairly squared-off tip. Or the secondaries might bulge like a weight lifter's biceps, as in the red-tailed hawk. The trailing edge of the wing may curve gracefully to a narrow hand, as in Swainson's hawk, or the leading edge may reach forward at the wrist, as in the sharp-shinned hawk. With practice and careful observation, hawks can often be identified before a single plumage mark is seen.

HOW TO READ THE MAPS

Range maps provide a simplified picture of a species' distribution. They indicate the birds that can be expected at any locality at different times of the year. Birds of prey are not evenly distributed over their ranges. To be present at all, they require habitat that will sustain both themselves and their prey. They are typically scarcest at their range limits, which are somewhat arbitrary, since a few individuals of many species inevitably wander far outside the ranges mapped.

Some raptors live year-round in the same locality, but many are migratory. In spring, they fly north to their nesting territories. In fall, they return south to their wintering grounds. Some birds that nest in the US and Canada winter in Mexico or farther south.

MAP KEY

SUMMER OR
NESTING

WINTER

ALL YEAR

MIGRATION
(spring & fall)

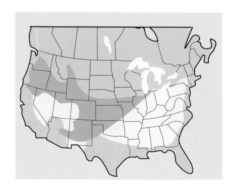

HOW THE BIRDS ARE ORGANIZED

TURKEY VULTURE

BLACK VULTURE

Black vultures are not as buoyant as turkey vultures and require stronger thermals for soaring. Sometimes they remain grounded when turkey vultures are aloft.

Often seen tugging at a piece of roadkill, vultures are large blackish birds with unfeathered heads—the "buzzards" of the old West. Their bare, wrinkled heads; dull, disheveled plumage; and carrion-eating habits create a sense of disgust in most people, not the awe inspired by hawks and eagles.

Vultures with red heads are adult turkey vultures. Black vultures and young turkey vultures have dark heads and can be confused with one another, but the black vulture is more compact and has a short tail that barely extends beyond the folded wing of a standing bird. Turkey vultures, young and old, are rangier birds with longer tails.

When not feeding, groups of vultures usually soar overhead, searching for carrion when weather permits. Sometimes they soar in lazy circles a few hundred feet above the ground, but on clear sunny days when strong thermals are produced, they will ascend as high as 2 miles and command a view of over 100 square miles. At that height, they can't see carrion on the ground; they watch the movements of nearby birds. Any bird that spots carrion and descends will draw the rest of the group to it.

Beyond a half mile, a soaring vulture is not visible to the naked eye. Even with binoculars, it is just a speck in the sky. Still, the shape of the distant speck can have enough definition to be identifiable. Black vultures may appear almost tailless, the stubbiness of their tails emphasized by being fanned. Turkey vultures have obvious tails, which they often hold closed even when soaring. It is the tiny head that often seems to be missing on a distant turkey vulture.

YOUNG CONDOR IN FLIGHT

ADULT CALIFORNIA CONDOR

The California condor is being nurtured back from near extinction. Young birds (which have dark heads) from captive breeding programs have been reintroduced in Los Padres National Forest of California and at the Grand Canyon.

Another mark often visible near the limit of sight is the flight style. Turkey vultures hold their wings above horizontal in a shallow V and rock from side to side as they soar. Black vultures hold their wings flat and regularly give a short series of quick, shallow flaps to maintain altitude.

The silvery white wing tips of the black vulture are a sure plumage mark visible from a long distance. All the flight feathers on the turkey vulture's underwing are silvery and contrast with the darker body, although the contrast may not always appear as obvious as it is shown in the illustration.

At most but not all **hawkwatches,** turkey vultures are widespread and common migrants. They are rare at northern sites from the Rockies east across the plains to the Great Lakes, and they are relatively scarce at most western Great Lakes sites.

Black vultures are mostly nonmigratory residents of the Southeast and are seen only incidentally from hawkwatch sites. However, they have been occurring with increasing frequency at sites in the Northeast as their range expands northward.

At a distance, both vultures can be confused with two more eagerly anticipated big, black migrants—the bald eagle and the golden eagle (p. 28). Neither eagle rocks like the turkey vulture, nor does either have a short tail and white wing tips like the black vulture.

Turkey vultures are on the move north as early as February. At most sites, spring migration peaks in mid-April, a bit earlier in the South. And they are among the last raptors to head south, peaking in the last half of October in the East and with significant numbers occurring well into November.

Vulture records have shown a steady recent increase, primarily because of the availability of roadkill, especially deer. Hundreds of thousands of deer perish annually in collisions with cars. Turkey vultures now account for about 25 percent of all spring migrants at many sites in the Southwest and on the eastern Great Lakes. Their numbers are large but their percentages smaller along the coasts.

young

Turkey Vulture

black
turkey

Black Vulture

OSPREY

CRESTED CARACARA

Ospreys and caracaras have little in common with each other and not much more in common with other raptors. Their foraging styles, structural adaptations, and appearance are all substantially different from those of other raptors, making identification relatively easy and straightforward.

Ospreys, mature and young alike, are extensively white below and have white heads with a sporty dark eye stripe. Many individuals, once thought to be females, have a necklace of fine brown breast streaks. In flight, a large dark patch at the bend of each wing contrasts distinctively with the white underparts. The dark feathers on young birds are tipped with white, producing a scalloped pattern on the mantle.

Ospreys are almost exclusively fish hawks that live near the coast or open inland waters. Only in migration are they seen far from water, and even then the highest concentrations are seen along the coastlines. They build huge, exposed nesting platforms of sticks and debris on the tops of trees or man-made structures such as utility poles and return to the same nest each year. Colonies form at locations with abundant food and nest sites.

Bald eagles (p. 28) also take fish, but not as adeptly as an osprey. A bald eagle prefers a fish that washes ashore or one stolen from an osprey to one that it has to capture itself. Flying low, a bald eagle swipes its talons through the water to grasp a fish at the surface, avoiding immersion if possible. Ospreys hover high over the water until locating their prey, fish that weigh about a pound and are within 2 or 3 feet of the surface. Then they dive. The dive is dramatic—at a steep angle from an average of 70 feet high and at high speed. They hit the water talons first and, more than half the time, emerge with their prey, dripping water as they fly to a nearby perch to consume it.

Caracaras eat prey that they can run down. They are especially fond of carrion (which can't run away) but subdue snakes and small animals as well. They sometimes search for prey from the wing in low, direct flight, but they always approach on foot.

The caracara doesn't migrate and won't be seen at hawk-watching sites. They are residents of open areas—grasslands, deserts, and pastures. In Texas, they are fairly numerous, but they are scarce in Arizona, and the Florida population has diminished with development and is now only about 500 birds.

Its unique habits, shape, and plumage make the crested caracara an easy bird to identify.

The vulture-like bare facial skin (which can be red or yellow) is evidence of its scavenging ways. A caracara is aggressive and will dominate vultures at a carcass. It is not a member of the vulture family. Surprisingly, it is closely related to the falcons.

The traditional osprey identification marks mentioned previously are seldom noted by experienced viewers at a **hawkwatch.** They yell "Osprey!" when they first note the distinctive wing shape and wing set of a distant bird. The wing shape suggests that of a gull—long, narrow, and jutting forward at the bend of the wing. In a glide or a soar, as typically seen, the inner wings are set upward; the outer wings droop. When they are carrying a fish, as happens occasionally, ospreys are even easier to identify. Several ospreys are often seen in sequence on the same flight path.

Like ospreys, many other hawk species tend to follow distinct routes by a hawkwatch, routes that are best suited for their flight styles under the prevailing weather conditions.

At least a few ospreys are recorded at most hawkwatch sites. They seldom account for more than a few percent of the total. Hawk Mountain, PA, records the highest numbers of any inland site, around 500 each fall. Cape May, NJ, on the coast, has recorded more than that in a day and averages tenfold more birds a season.

Spring migration begins in late March, with the peak occurring from mid-April to the first week of May. Fall peak is mid- to late September.

26

bald eagle
harassing
osprey

Osprey

caracara

Crested Caracara

black vulture
(p. 20)

heir magnificent size sets eagles apart from hawks. Even a small male will have a 6-foot wingspan; a female's often exceeds 7 feet. By comparison, the largest hawks span about 4 1/2 feet, wing tip to wing tip. Only turkey vultures and ospreys approach an eagle's wingspan.

GOLDEN EAGLE

BLAD EAGLE

Adult eagles are easy to distinguish from each other—the golden doesn't have the white head and tail of the bald eagle. It has a golden nape (which can look white in strong light) that contrasts with its chocolate brown body. It is young eagles that make identification challenging, and they can be separated at a good distance if you know what to look for.

The young bald eagle illustrated on p. 31 is typical of a first- or second-year bird. With each molt, the young birds become whiter until becoming completely dark below in their fourth year.

Young golden eagles usually have white patches at the base of their outer flight feathers. The patches may be larger than shown or smaller. They sometimes are narrow and extend to the body in a thin line, but they are always on the flight feathers, never on the coverts that cover the forewing or on the body.

Young bald eagles show a widely varying amount of white below. They always have white wing pits (base of the wing, next to the body) where the golden eagle never shows white. Sometimes little more than the wing pit is white on very young bald eagles, but usually white extends in rough bars toward the wing tip along the forewing—not on the flight feathers, although the flight feathers often have ill-defined white areas as well. During their second full year, bald eagles are extensively white below, including the belly.

Young eagles of both species have white tails with a dark terminal band. The band is usually well defined in young goldens, less so in young balds. It is also more variable in young bald eagles: wide on younger birds, narrow on older ones. A narrow dark terminal band is the only indication of youth on fourth-year bald eagles; the rest of the plumage is like an adult's.

Bald eagles are opportunistic feeders. Most congregate near water and feed on fish, which they catch, scavenge, or steal from others, including ospreys. They also take waterfowl or whatever else presents itself as an easy catch. Golden eagles, on the other hand, are true hunters, taking mostly small mammals. They hunt from a soar and, in hilly areas, by coursing low to the ground and surprising prey by suddenly appearing from behind the terrain.

The golden eagle migration in spring along the front range of the Rocky Mountains was only recently discovered. Bridger Mountain, MT; Mount Head, Alberta; and Mount Lorette, Alberta, all record from 1,000 to 4,000 annually.

Except in southern Texas, bald eagles are seen annually at North American **hawkwatches.** Hawk Ridge, MN, tallies a few thousand each year. Golden eagles are numerous in the West, especially at sites in the northern Rockies.

Hawkwatch sites
have documented
both the decline of
bald eagles due to
pesticide poisoning in
the 1960s and '70s
and their current
recovery.

Although the golden eagle was extirpated over much of the East, a small but increasing population nesting in northeastern Canada is seen in migration at many eastern hawkwatches.

Eagles are early migrants in spring, peaking in March at most sites, and are late migrants in fall, with the peak usually occurring in November. In the East, a second pulse of northbound bald eagles occurs in May and June, and an early southbound pulse in August and September. These are early-nesting southeastern birds and their offspring, which wander north in summer.

A bird the size of an eagle is often first seen as a small fixed dot in the distance. Smaller birds are not seen until they are nearer the observer, and their apparent size increases more rapidly as they close. Turkey vultures are sometimes transformed into eagles by hopeful hawk-watchers, but eagles never teeter in flight like turkey vultures. Some young bald eagles with extensively white underparts and heads also show a dark osprey-like eye stripe and can be initially mistaken for ospreys (p. 24).

A bald eagle has distinctively deeper wing beats than a golden eagle or buteo, and its large head and bill extends half or more the distance before the wing than its tail extends behind. The head of a golden eagle is closer to one-third of the tail extension.

young

Golden
Eagle

golden

young

bald

young

Bald Eagle

RED-TAILED HAWK

RED-TAILED HAWK

KRIDER'S RED-TAILED HAWK

HARLAN'S RED-TAILED HAWK

A t all seasons and across the breadth of the US and southern Canada, the one large hawk most often seen is the red-tailed. It is the hawk commonly seen perched on a roadside fence post or utility pole. It is the hawk most often seen soaring overhead at midday. (It is not the hawk that harasses backyard birds. These are accipiters, p. 62). It is the hawk to which all other buteos are compared because it is the easiest with which to gain familiarity.

Red-tails proliferate because they are adaptable, requiring only a patch of woodland for shelter and open fields in which to hunt. In the Southwest, saguaro cactus suffices for shelter. Red-tails aren't fussy about prey, either, although rodents are the common meal. They adapt to whatever hunting style succeeds with the prey at hand. They are one of the few hawks capable of "kiting," or hanging in the wind over suspected prey without flapping.

The red-tailed is also the most variable hawk. There are seven races and six distinct forms, not including intermediates and young birds. All the variety occurs in the West and Midwest; only one form is regular in the East.

The eastern-form adult, which also occurs in the West, has sure marks when seen from any angle. The brick red tail with a dark band

32

near the tip is the best mark from the back side of a perched bird, but also note the white V-shaped mottling across the back. The extent of the mottling varies with the individual.

From the front, the creamy white chest and belly are apparent, with a distinctive contrasting belly band. The belly band is composed of parallel vertical strokes and is quite variable. The strokes can be thin or thick, dense or widely spaced, but they are always there to some extent on eastern-form birds. The tail, seen from the front, is a pale pink.

The belly band and pink underside of the tail are also visible on flying adults. However, two dark patches on the forewing are the best marks. One is a narrow dark strip along the leading edge of the wing, near the body (patagial mark); the other, a dark comma-shaped mark just past the bend of the wing.

The namesake red tail is a good mark for all adult forms of the red-tailed hawk in the West, except Harlan's and Krider's. Fuerte's form of the red-tail, common in the Southwest, is like the eastern form but lacks the belly band and the white mottling on the back. The other western forms have numerous fine dark bands on their red tails, not just one near the tip. The most widespread western red-tail is similar to the eastern form except for the tail bands and tawnier underparts. Some western birds are very dark bodied, usually reddish brown but occasionally nearly black. The belly band and forewing marks can be obscured on dark-form birds, but their tails reveal their identity.

Young birds of the forms already described are marked like adults except on the tails. There is usually no red in a young bird's tail. It is brown above and pale below, with fine dark bands on both sides.

Krider's and Harlan's hawks are so distinctive that they were once considered separate species. Krider's is scarce, a bird of the Great Plains, but similar individuals are seen in the Far West. Think of it as a washed-out eastern-form bird, whiter above, below, and even on the tail, where only a terminal band of pink is normally seen. Only the ferruginous hawk (p. 42) is similar, having a pinkish terminal band to its white tail. Krider's is much whiter above than the ferruginous and, on the underwing, shows the distinctive forewing patches of a red-tail. Young Krider's have tan tails with fine dark bands.

Harlan's hawk is fairly numerous in winter on prairies. The adult is difficult to distinguish from a blackish red-tail except for the tail. Harlan's is a red-tail without a red tail. The typical Harlan's tail is dirty white at the base, with dark streaks (not bands!) creating a marbled effect and

Dark-form red-tails account for 10 percent or more of the flight at many western hawkwatches. At Hawk Mountain, PA, in the East and Enger Tower, MN, along the Great Lakes, dark-form birds are only 1 percent of those recorded. A single Krider's or Harlan's hawk is cause for celebration at any hawkwatch.

34

blending to a thin dark band near the tip. Some birds have darker tails than others, and a few are nearly white above except for the sub-terminal band. The scarce dark form of the rough-legged hawk (p. 42) can have a similar tail but never with marbling. Harlan's also shows white flecks on the mantle, underwings, and especially the breast that are seldom seen on rough-legs or dark-form red-tails. Young Harlan's have tails like young dark-form red-tails. Separating the two is a job for experts.

At two sites in the proximity of Winnipeg, Manitoba—one close to St. Adolphe and the other near Windygates, about 90 percent of the spring flight is red-tails. Windygates has recorded 3,671 in one spring day. Derby Hill, NY, holds the record with 4,591.

Red-tails migrate early in spring, peaking in late March or early April. They are numerous along the Pacific coast and at most interior **hawkwatch sites,** less so along the Atlantic coast. More than 75 percent of the count at Cape Flattery, WA, is red-tails. Fall migration is prolonged in the West, peaking in October. In the East, fall migration is late, peaking in late October or early November with over 500 birds on peak days at many watches, "beak-to-tail," as veterans like to describe the parade.

At hawkwatches that provide eye-level views, oncoming red-tails can be spotted by their "landing lights"—the white patches along the leading edge of the wing between the dark forewing bar and the comma.

Learning a red-tail's shape helps in recognizing other, rarer buteos. The adult red-tail is chunky, with broad wings, bulging secondaries (the trailing edge of the wing near the body), and a hand (the outer portion of the wing) that seems to reach forward in a soar. All other buteos, including young red-tails, are rangier.

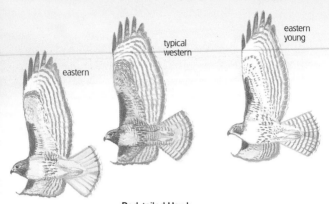

eastern

typical
western

eastern
young

Red-tailed Hawk

Fuerte's
form

eastern
form

typical
western
form

eastern
young

dark western

Krider's

Harlan's

dark western form

Krider's Hawk

Harlan's Hawk

SWAINSON'S HAWK

For a Swainson's hawk, home is a field of grass or crops, and the weather is always warm. To live that life, they migrate all the way from the prairies of central North America to the pampas of South America, a flight of up to 6,000 miles each way. The main pulse of migrants arrives in Texas in early April and reaches the Canadian prairies in early May. Most stay until late September or early October.

Most of the time, Swainson's hawks feed on insects, either catching them in the air or snatching them from the ground. Often they are seen clustered on the ground collecting grasshoppers and the like. However, nestlings are fed a typical hawk diet of rodents and other small animals. A grasshopper, cricket, or dragonfly is too small to be worth a trip to the nest. Mated adults will hunt small prey from a perch when one is available, and they often course slowly near the ground like harriers, rocking and hovering. Yearlings, which don't mate, feast on insects throughout the season.

Swainson's has a variety of plumages. One consistent and definitive feature found on adults and young birds alike is the dark flight feathers. They contrast especially prominently with the white underwings on pale-form Swainson's. Flight feathers are pale on all other hawks except a couple of southwestern rarities: Harris' hawk and the common black-hawk (p. 52). Tails are also very similar on all forms of Swainson's, gray or gray-brown with fine dark bands, a wide dark band near the tip, and a white tip. The base of the tail on some birds can be nearly white.

For convenience, Swainson's adult plumages are often divided into three forms, but in fact, the variations are nearly continuous. All the variation is on the underparts; upperparts are evenly dark. Pale-form birds are white below except for a red-brown bib and some spotting on the sides and lower breast. Dark-form individuals can have evenly dark underparts, but many are intermediate, showing a contrast between the darker bib and a reddish, heavily barred belly.

Dark-form Swainson's hawks are scarce in most of their range, but the proportion of dark birds increases to the west. In northeastern California, more than half are dark.

Veteran hawk-watcher and author Pete Dunne aptly likens a young Swainson's facial markings to chocolate dribblings extending down the cheeks onto the chest.

On young birds, plumage also varies from pale to dark and is quite distinct from that of adults. A pale-form bird in its first fall is cream or buff colored below, with heavy dark streaks running down the cheeks and breaking up into dark spotting on the breast and belly, especially on the sides. There is a very pale eyebrow and a dark eye line. The upper back is dark but heavily mottled with cream- to buff-colored spots. Darker birds are more heavily spotted below, especially on the breast. The following spring when the youngsters return to North America, their plumage is worn and sun-bleached white to varying degrees on pale-form birds. The head, breast, and even the upper back can be largely white, creating wide variations among individuals.

Most North American **hawkwatch sites** see Swainson's hawks in small numbers, if at all. Flocks of 10,000 are common where migrants are funneled through Central America. Large kettles are seen annually riding thermals in south Texas, but beyond there the funnel widens too much for large numbers to be seen reliably at any more northerly point.

Swainson's holds its wings in a V when it soars, and it rocks somewhat like a turkey vulture. Seen from below, the wings usually reach forward from the body and are more slender, tapered, and graceful than those of the red-tailed hawk. The tail is longer than a red-tail's.

A few Swainson's migrate through the East each fall, to the delight of eastern hawkwatchers. Usually more than 100 end up trapped in south Florida and the Keys each winter. Some 30 more winter in California's Sacramento–San Joaquin River delta.

pale

dark

Swainson's Hawk

intermediate

pale form
young

pale form

dark
form

PRAIRIE BUTEOS

FERRUGINOUS HAWK

ROUGH-LEGGED HAWK

In addition to hunting from a perch and coursing, ferruginous hawks occasionally hover like a rough-legged hawk over suspected prey.

carce hawks of open areas, the rough-leg and ferruginous also share the minor distinction of being the only buteos with legs feathered to the toes. Both are the size of a red-tail or larger and have longer, more slender wings. The ferruginous (rusty-colored) hawk is the largest buteo. Or is it the smallest eagle?

Because of its regal bearing, size, and similarities with the golden eagle, it has been speculated that the ferruginous is more eagle than buteo. It has the golden eagle's heavy wing flap, occupies similar habitat, and sometimes courses like a golden eagle, close to the ground, searching for prey such as prairie dogs, jackrabbits, squirrels, and grouse.

East of the Rockies, the ferruginous lives on short-grass plains and fields (especially of alfalfa); to the west, it also occupies sagebrush and desert. It frequently perches on the ground, poised and alert, waiting for a gopher or prairie dog to emerge from a burrow. Groups of ferruginous hawks may be seen standing at the outskirts of prairie dog colonies.

The rusty mantle, white tail blending to a reddish tip on the topside, and extensive white underparts make an adult pale-form ferruginous relatively easy to identify. Seen soaring, the reddish V of the legs contrasts with the white belly.

The ferruginous hawk is more massive than the red-tailed hawk, with a larger head and broader chest. At close range, the wide, yellow-lined gape (edges of the mouth) is obvious.

Also note the black comma near the bend of the wing. The comma is even visible on dark-form birds. A few percent of ferruginous hawks are dark form—brown to reddish below. Their tails are more gray than white at the base.

Young ferruginous hawks have buff breasts and several ill-defined gray bands on their tails. They lack the reddish leggings of adults.

Most rough-legged hawks are also relatively easy to identify, in spite of their variation. The dark blotch on the underwing at the bend of the wing is usually the easiest mark. It is visible on all but the darkest of dark-form birds. (About 20 percent are dark form.) Also note the white tail with a broad band near the tip; males have additional fine tail bands.

Young rough-legs have solid dark bellies and pale breasts with fine dark streaks. In adults, especially males, breast streaks are heavier and the belly band is mottled with white, often making the breast darker than the belly.

Rough-legs nest in the Arctic and are pushed south by cold weather to the marshes, fields, and prairies of the US. Their numbers explode and contract with the lemming population on which they feed when nesting, but they are never numerous. They hover over prey, which is almost exclusively rodents.

In migration, the largest numbers of rough-legs are seen at several Great Lakes **hawkwatches.** Over 1,000 have been seen at Hawk Ridge, MN, in fall and at Whitefish Point, MI, in spring. The fall numbers don't peak until November, and the main pulse in spring is not until late April. Although scarce or rare at hawkwatches east of the Great Lakes, rough-legs are the most likely dark-form hawk to pass; their silvery flight feathers can suggest a turkey vulture.

Rough-legs are less dependent on thermals than other buteos and are likely to be seen either late in the day or early, flying under their own power. When they soar, their wings rise in a V near the body but level out at the bend of the wing, not unlike a harrier's (p. 54). Rough-legs are chestier, broader winged, and shorter tailed than a harrier. However, they are lankier, with narrower wings and a longer tail, than the bulky, commonly seen red-tailed hawk.

Ferruginous hawks migrate over plains and grasslands, but some don't migrate at all. They are seldom seen even at favored hawk-watch sites. Perhaps two dozen pass in fall at the Goshutes, NV, site and at Golden Gate, CA. Bright white patches in their primaries combined with the white base of the tail can be seen as three "points of light" at great distances, an excellent mark.

pale form

young

ferruginous

rough-leg

dark ♂

pale ♀

young

Rough-legged Hawk

Ferruginous Hawk

pale form ♂

pale form

young

WOODLAND BUTEOS

RED-SHOULDERED HAWK

BROAD-WINGED HAWK

Red-shouldered hawks often announce their presence with a distinctive *kee-yah* call. When trying to locate the source of a call, don't be surprised to find a blue jay being a mimic.

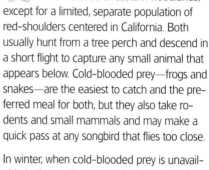

Red-shouldered and broad-winged hawks are birds of eastern woodlands, except for a limited, separate population of red-shoulders centered in California. Both usually hunt from a tree perch and descend in a short flight to capture any small animal that appears below. Cold-blooded prey—frogs and snakes—are the easiest to catch and the preferred meal for both, but they also take rodents and small mammals and may make a quick pass at any songbird that flies too close.

In winter, when cold-blooded prey is unavailable in the north, some red-shoulders rely on rodents and ambush small birds as an accipiter (p. 62) does. Most withdraw from the northern portion of their range and concentrate to the south. Broad-wings leave the US entirely in winter, except for a few stragglers trapped in south Florida.

Although their summer ranges, habitat, and choice of prey overlap, the broad-wing is most numerous in the northern US and southern Canada, whereas the red-shoulder's largest numbers are in the South, especially in swamps. The red-shoulder likes large sections of mature woodlands with an open understory in which to perch and hunt. Broad-wings accept younger, more fragmented forest with denser ground cover. They typically use a

46

perch at the edge of a clearing for hunting. Both birds are attracted to streams and wetlands by the prey to be found there, but they are also seen in upland forest far from water.

Both the broad-wing and red-shoulder are small buteos. The red-shoulder is about 20 percent smaller than a red-tailed hawk, and the broad-wing, smaller yet. Red-shouldered hawks, indeed, have red or, more precisely, chestnut shoulders, but broad-winged hawks do not have especially broad wings for a buteo; in fact, the hand is gently tapered.

The tail and the upper surface of the red-shoulder's flight feathers are black-and-white striped. When the wing is folded, the stripes are transformed into a houndstooth pattern. Adult broad-wings have fewer tail bands, and the white bands are as wide as the dark ones, not narrower, as on a red-shoulder's tail. There is also a broad dark band on the trailing edge of the underwing of adult broad-wings.

Young red-shoulders and broad-wings are streaked with brown below rather than barred with chestnut, similar to a young Cooper's hawk (p. 62). The streaking is more extensive on a young red-tail; concentrated at the sides in a young broad-wing. The red shoulders can be faint on a young red-shoulder, but its tail pattern is distinctly different from a young

Broad-wings are secretive when nesting, and so are red-shoulders in their northern range. In other areas and in winter, the red-shoulder often perches openly. In California, it is regularly seen along major highways.

Red-shouldered hawks in California and Florida are a bit different from the typical form illustrated. Florida birds, and some in nearby states, are noticeably smaller and paler, with a grayer head and back.

The birds in California are also smaller than the typical red-shoulder. They have solid reddish breasts and fewer, wider white tail bands.

broad-wing's. Broad-wings have a dark band near the tail tip that is twice the width of the other dark bands.

Broad-winged hawk migration is the foremost spectacle at many eastern and Great Lakes **hawkwatch sites**. By mid-September, several thousand may be counted on big days. In late September, when they converge in Texas, daily flights reach the tens of thousands. Kettles of one hundred or more birds rising on a midday thermal are common. Spring migration peaks in late April and early May. Small numbers of broad-wings, including some rare dark-form birds, migrate along the Rockies and the Pacific coast.

The timing of the broad-winged migration—late in spring, early in fall—is determined by the availability of their cold-blooded prey.

Red-shouldered hawks are most numerous at Great Lakes hawkwatch sites. Spring migration here peaks as early as the end of March; fall migration may not peak until early November. Cape May, NJ, and Hawk Mountain, PA, see hundreds each season, but smaller numbers are typical at other eastern sites.

Red-shouldered hawks often fly point to point with fast wing beats, like an accipiter. When they soar, their wings reach forward. Broad-wings stick their wings straight out.

Crescent-shaped "windows" just inside the dark tips of the red-shoulder's wings are good marks for backlit birds and can be seen at long distances. Light passes through these windows and illuminates them—white in adults, tawny in young birds. Other hawks have similar windows, but they are rarely crescent shaped.

48

young

red-shouldered

broad-winged

young

Red-shouldered Hawk

Broad-winged Hawk

young

young

SHORT-TAILED HAWK

WHITE-TAILED HAWK

Only perhaps 1,000 white-tailed hawks nest in the US, and just half as many short-tails. Short-tails migrate within Florida; white-tails are Texas residents.

ale-form short-tailed hawks resemble white-tailed hawks. They share an uncanny ability to hang motionless in the sky while scanning for prey below, and they often soar very high. However, they don't share air space. Short-tails hunt over woodland edges in peninsular Florida, using their impressive flying skills to take birds. White-tails soar over Texas coastal grassland and interior scrub seeking small ground animals.

Usually seen far aloft, short-tails can be identified by their flat wing set with distinctively curled tips. Adult dark-form short-tails, the more numerous form, have solid dark underparts; pale-form birds are white below. The adult's wings have a broad dark trailing edge, and there is a wide dark band near the tip of the adult's tail, often with several narrower bands toward the base. Young birds have more tail bands, and the young dark form has white mottling on its belly and wing linings.

The white tail and underparts of an adult white-tailed hawk are set off distinctively by its broad dark tail band. Note the chestnut shoulder patch on perched birds. Young birds are dark below except for a white splotch on the chest, white cheeks, and some white mottling on the wing linings. Their flight feathers and tails are finely banded.

50

short-tailed

white-tailed

pale form

young

dark form
young

young

White-tailed Hawk

Short-tailed Hawk

young

dark form

pale form

pale form
young

SOUTHERN BUTEOS

HARRIS' HAWK

ZONE-TAILED HAWK

COMMON BLACK-HAWK

There are about 50 pairs of gray hawks along streams in southeastern Arizona, southwestern New Mexico, and the Rio Grande Valley. All plumages show a white U-shaped rump band.

Three tropical buteos in addition to the white-tailed hawk (p. 50) ignore the US-Mexican border and extend their range into Texas and the American Southwest. Harris' hawk is a fairly numerous resident. Zone-tailed hawks and common black-hawks are scarcer; most breach the border only to nest.

Harris' hawk often hunts in family groups and takes a variety of prey. The chestnut shoulder, leggings, and wing linings of the adult are easy marks; so is the black-banded tail. The chestnut markings on young birds are fainter but sufficient to be recognized.

On a perch, zone-tails and adult black-hawks are bulky black birds resembling one another. However, the black-hawk has a white band on both surfaces of its tail. The upper tail surface of the zone-tail is banded in gray. Young black-hawks are buff below and heavily streaked; their tails are buff, with numerous dark bands.

In flight, the zone-tail mimics the look and flight of a turkey vulture. The disguise allows it to closely approach and capture the swift birds and lizards that are its primary prey. Black-hawks prefer not to fly at all; they sit. They perch on a branch over a shallow stream or stand at its edge, like a heron, until a fish, frog, snake, or other small prey presents itself.

common
black-hawk

young

zone-tailed

♂

young

young

Harris'

Zone-tailed Hawk

Harris' Hawk

NORTHERN HARRIER

SWALLOW-TAILED KITE

The remaining strongholds of the swallow-tailed kite are the undeveloped portions of south-western Florida and coastal South Carolina.

Swallow-tailed kites grace the skies with a beauty beyond that of any other raptor. They are the most distinctive and quickly identified bird of prey. Unfortunately, there aren't many left to identify. They once ranged along the Mississippi River and its major tributaries as far north as Ohio and Minnesota. By the mid-1900s, habitat loss and shooting had reduced their range to its present limits, and their numbers to about 1,000 nesting pairs.

Harriers are very distinctive raptors also. The basis of their distinction shows in their faces. They have owl-like facial discs for the same reason that owls have them, to pinpoint prey by sound. Their sight and their flying skills are keen as well. Male harriers (smaller than females) are such agile hunters that they subsist entirely on birds in some localities.

Harriers live in open lands, usually marshes in the East, also dry uplands in the West. They don't require trees for nesting and seldom perch on limbs; a fence, a rise in the ground, or a muskrat house will do. They are often first recognized by their hunting style—gliding and tipping a few yards above the ground in slow, buoyant flight as they use eyes and ears to register the movement of anything below. Wings are held in a shallow V. A prominent white rump patch confirms the identification.

Except for the rump patch, male and female harriers have separate plumages. Adult males are blue-gray above and extensively white below, with contrasting black wing tips. Adult females are brown above and tawny below, with dark streaking. They weigh more than males by half, on average, and are several inches longer. Young birds are brown above, like females, but have rusty-colored breasts.

Swallow-tailed kites—male and female, young and adult—have the same black-and-white plumage and are the same size except for a noticeably shorter tail on young birds. It is the tail surface, constantly flexed and twisted, that a kite often uses to direct its flight as it slips through the air on fixed wings or hangs in a near-motionless stall.

Swallow-tailed kites lack the orbital ridge that protrudes over the eye and distinguishes most raptors. It gives their faces a much gentler look.

Swallow-tailed kites are usually aloft during the day, feeding on insects. They don't perch to eat or drink. They catch flying insects and also slowly glide over a treetop or canopy and pluck them from the foliage. Like Swainson's hawk (p. 38), another insect specialist, adults capture more substantial meals—frogs, snakes, nestling birds—to take to the nest to feed their young.

Only a few wandering swallow-tailed kites are seen at **hawkwatches.** Swallow-tails are migrants, but they migrate from the tropics to the southern shores of the US, not much farther inland. They first arrive in southwestern Florida in late February and are gone again by mid-September. Hundreds gather in communal roosts in the Everglades in late July and August, prior to migration. Some apparently migrate directly over the Gulf; others island-hop down the Caribbean; and a very few take the traditional raptor routes through Mexico.

Harriers are seen at hawkwatches throughout the US and southern Canada, especially along the Atlantic coast, where Cape May, NJ, averages more than 1,500 per year. Their migration is more prolonged than the typical raptor's. Spring passage begins in the Southwest in late February and finishes in Canada around the start of May, with adults preceding the young of the previous year. Peak numbers can occur early or late in the season. Fall migration runs from mid-August to late November, with young birds preceding adults by an average of about one month.

The harrier's white rump patch shows well at long distances and is a good mark at hawkwatches. The V set of the wings on soaring and gliding birds is a good early mark as well. Harriers have slender bodies and wings. They fly buoyantly and often unsteadily, with a few easy wing strokes and a glide.

Harriers display their flight mastery in spring courtship displays with spectacular dives, loops, and rolls.

young

♀

harrier

♂

Northern Harrier

♂

♀

Swallow-tailed Kite

WHITE-TAILED KITE

MISSISSIPPI KITE

White-tailed kites are most often seen hover-hunting early and late in the day.

L ike the swallow-tailed kite (p. 54), the white-tailed and Mississippi kites hunt conspicuously, each with its own signature style. A white-tailed kite hunts from a hover. It picks a spot 20 to 80 feet above promising terrain and hovers, sometimes a minute or more, while it scans the ground for the movement of small rodents. If it finds nothing, it flies to another spot and repeats the process. When a vole or mouse is spotted, it doesn't dive or swoop as another hawk might, but descends feet first, using its wings like a parachute to control the rate of fall.

White-tailed kites lost range in the early 1900s but have reclaimed it. From their stronghold in California, nesting pairs have spread to Oregon and Washington. Expansion from their east Texas range has largely been into Mexico and Central America, but they have nested in Florida (continuously since 1986) and occasionally on the Gulf Coast. Open grasslands, wetlands, and fields are favorite haunts. They sometimes hover-hunt along a fencerow or irrigation ditch. In California, they work the margins of highways. They don't usually hunt together or nest in colonies, but like other kites, they are very social, roosting in flocks except when nesting.

Mississippi kites sail and glide through the skies taking flying insects. Blue sky—that is, bug-infested blue sky—is their true habitat. They fly over plains or forest, remote areas or suburbs, wherever grasshoppers, dragonflies, cicadas, and the like are available. Their numbers and range are increasing. A few wanderers are reported each year far north of their established range.

Like swallow-tailed kites, Mississippi kites often feed with their own kind, constantly shifting their tails to perform the aerial maneuvers leading to an insect's capture. They differ from swallow-tails by typically flying higher and gliding faster rather than skimming the treetops in slow flight and gleaning insects from vegetation.

All adult kites are distinctive combinations of white, black, and shades of gray. The small exception is the red eye, a glowing ember in the coal-black eye patch of both the white-tailed and Mississippi kites.

SNAIL KITE

About 500 snail kites live in south Florida. They have little in common with other North American kites. They feed almost exclusively on fresh-water snails and move to wherever water levels make the snails available.

Both its white tail and black shoulder are easy marks for the the white-tailed kite (once named the black-shouldered kite). The underwing pattern is also distinctive. Young birds resemble adults except for a rusty-colored wash on their heads and breasts.

Mississippi kites have never been formally known as black-tailed kites or white-winged kites, but for identification, either would have been a good name. The adult's white wing panels can appear even brighter and more obvious than illustrated. Females have darker backs than males. Young birds in their first fall are sandy brown to chocolate above and heavily streaked below; their black tails have narrow translucent (not opaque white) bands. Young birds returning in spring resemble adults but retain their immature tails and wings and have varying amounts of streaking below.

Handfuls of white-tailed kites are seen at **hawkwatches** in south Texas and at the Golden Gate, CA, hawkwatch. They are better considered wanderers than true migrants. Mississippi kites are true migrants; great flocks are seen along the east coast of Mexico and Texas. Thousands pass over Santa Anna NWR in spring and fall. They arrive in mid-April, just as their insect prey is becoming prevalent, and they leave in late August and early September.

Both the white-tailed and Mississippi kites have a falcon-like shape, and the plumage of a young Mississippi can be confused with that of a young peregrine falcon (p. 70). However,. peregrines usually fly powerfully or, on occasion, soar. Kites glide, flapping only as a last resort and seldom soaring. A small but useful mark for the Mississippi kite is the very short outer flight feather.

Because they are such wanderers, kites can show up at nearly any hawkwatch in late summer or early fall. Approaching from a distance, a Mississippi kite may appear all dark except for the contrasting pale head of the adult. Young tundra peregrines with extensively blond napes and heads can also look pale headed.

white-tailed

Mississippi

young
in spring

young in fall

White-tailed Kite

Mississippi Kite

young

young

COOPER'S HAWK

SHARP-SHINNED HAWK

Cooper's and the sharp-shin regularly try to ambush birds at backyard feeders, particularly in winter. Their prey are usually well aware of the danger, and it is usually the least fit that are taken.

Cooper's and sharp-shinned hawks are so similar that they are easily and often mistaken for each other. Both are woodland inhabitants that live primarily by ambushing smaller birds, although Cooper's hawk also regularly takes squirrels and chipmunks. They perch quietly until an unsuspecting bird gets too close, or they stealthily course through woodlands attempting to surprise a bird at close range. Starlings, jays, and robins are among Cooper's favorite avian prey. Sharp-shins prefer smaller songbirds: sparrows, finches, and warblers.

Their secretive ways make Cooper's and sharp-shins difficult to identify. They typically flush from a tree at close range (but before being seen) and disappear as a blur into the under-story, leaving the almost-viewer wondering, "What was that?" If it was between the size of a blue jay and a crow, chances are good it was a sharp-shinned or Cooper's hawk. Blue-gray blurs are adults; brown blurs, young birds.

It is easier to get a good look at both accipiters at hawkwatches, but they are still difficult to separate from each other. If binoculars could be accurately calibrated across their field of vision, separating Cooper's from a sharp-shin would be easy. And males could be distinguished from females just as certainly, for

Sharp-shins are more numerous than Cooper's hawks, but in the East, the majority nest farther north than Cooper's, in unpopulated surroundings. In most of the West, where nesting ranges overlap, Cooper's are more common than sharp-shins.

there is no size overlap. Male sharp-shins are the smallest, about the size of a blue jay; females are larger, but smaller than a male Cooper's. Female Cooper's are the largest, about the size of a crow. It is the birds that are bigger than a blue jay but smaller than a crow that are hard to name.

The tail is a good mark. Tails on both species are banded, but Cooper's has a narrow white tip, and the tip shape is round; that is, the outer tail feathers are shorter than the middle ones. Tails on both birds appear rounded when they are spread. Sharp-shins have a very narrow, often gray tail tip, and the tail is squared off, or nearly so. An adult male Cooper's hawk, the sex closest in size to a sharp-shin, also has a dark cap that contrasts with its back. There is no distinct contrast between cap and back in adult sharp-shins.

Young birds are the same size as adults but have a different plumage, which offers an additional clue. The streaked underparts of the two birds are subtly different. Young sharp-shins are more heavily and evenly streaked. Streaking is finer on young Cooper's and is densest at the neck, less so on the belly. The effect is well illustrated in the flying images on p. 65.

Good to abundant numbers of sharp-shins are seen at nearly all **hawkwatches** across the continent. Cooper's hawks are far fewer except at some western sites. The migration is protracted, from the last half of March through the first half of May in spring and throughout September and October in fall. Cape May, NJ, catches the biggest flights. A good day there will record Cooper's hawks in the hundreds and more than a thousand sharp-shins.

Accipiters are distinguished from other hawks by their long banded tails, relatively short round wings, and typical flight style—several flaps and a glide. Being able to reliably separate migrating Cooper's from sharp-shins earns a measure of respect at any hawk-watch. The identification problem is further complicated by the welcome possibility of a young goshawk (p. 66).

At a distance, check the shape first. In a soar, Cooper's wings extend straight from the body; the sharp-shin's have a curved leading edge and are relatively broader. The curve makes the sharp-shin's head appear tucked in like a turtle's, emphasizing its smaller size. Overall, Cooper's is lankier than the sharp-shin, and its white rounded tail tip is visible at close range.

On a young Cooper's, the underparts appear mostly pale at long distance except for a dark head and upper breast. The young sharp-shin's heavy streaking makes it look darker below.

ADULTS IN TYPICAL FLIGHT; YOUNG, SOARING

TYPICAL VARIATIONS IN SHARP-SHINNED HAWK'S TAIL

sharp-shinned young ♂

Cooper's young

Cooper's young ♂

sharp-shinned young

young

Cooper's Hawk

young

Sharp-shinned Hawk

young

GOSHAWK

GYRFALCON

Gyrs and goshawks are prized by falconers. In the Middle Ages, when falconry was the rage among nobility, gyrs were flown only by the most privileged. Nearly all gyrs flown today are captive-bred birds

Goshawks are the largest of the accipiters; gyrfalcons, the grandest of the falcons. Both are powerful hunters—opportunists capable of taking prey the size of geese. Neither bothers with insects, frogs, or the other easy pickings favored by many raptors.

The two birds have different hunting styles. Like other accipiters, goshawks are woodland birds that ambush prey, either from a concealed perch or by coursing close to the ground. They like mature forest with an open understory, but they often hunt in clearings. When a snowshoe hare, grouse, squirrel, or similar-size prey is sighted, they give chase with determination and aggressiveness that are legendary. Prey is bowled over, grasped with the talons, and dispatched by repeated "footing" until a vital organ is pierced.

Gyrfalcons have such speed and power that they can hunt in open spaces. They simply overpower the ptarmigan, which is their common prey. (Near coasts, they often take waterbirds.) Gyrfalcons typically ball up their toes and smack large prey with a single devastating blow. Even a fast-flying duck (traveling 60 mph or more) will be driven to the ground in exhaustion if not overtaken and knocked from the sky. The kill is complete when a specialized notch in the gyr's bill severs the prey's vertebrae.

66

No one knows how many, or how few, gyrfalcons (JEER-falcons) live in the Arctic, but an informed estimate is that there are perhaps only 5,000 in North America.

Both goshawks and gyrfalcons are birds of the Far North, although some goshawks inhabit mountain forests in the West. Most gyrfalcons nest north of the arctic tree line. Many retreat at least to the tree line in winter, and a very few winter regularly in the northern tier of states. In most inhabited areas, however, a reported gyrfalcon is big news among birders and attracts large numbers of hopeful viewers.

Goshawks are common in the US only in comparison to gyrfalcons. In winter, some goshawks move to the northern US, and western birds drop to lower elevations, where they are more readily seen. About every ten years, when snowshoe hares and grouse are at a cyclical low point, large numbers of goshawks are forced south to find food. The cycle has been regular, with invasions peaking in the winters of 1972-73, 1982-83, and 1992-93.

Goshawks and gyrfalcons are similar in size to the red-tailed hawk (p. 32), and males are smaller than females. Like other accipiters, goshawks have broad tails with several bands, and young birds are brown above and streaked below. The adult's blue-gray upperparts, pale gray underparts, and white eyebrow are clinching marks. The eyebrow is less prominent on young birds. Good marks separating them from a young Cooper's (p. 62) are the hint of a tawny shoulder bar and dirtier-looking underparts with broader, blurrier streaks.

Adult gyrfalcons vary from white birds with some dark flecking above to dark birds that are gray-brown above and heavily barred below. Young birds are darker yet. Males are smaller than some large peregrines (p. 70) but lack a peregrine's distinctive helmet-like sideburns. Only a faint mustache mark shows on the gyr.

A passing gyrfalcon is a very rare event at any **hawkwatch.** Some goshawks—mostly young birds—do migrate, however, and in invasion years, many adults join them. Hawk Ridge, MN, and the Goshutes, NV, are the only places that regularly see more than 100 in fall. In an invasion year, Hawk Ridge counts from 1,000 to 5,000 goshawks. Peak fall migration is from late October to early November. In spring, several Great Lakes sites will record a few dozen goshawks from late March to early May.

An approaching goshawk is often mistaken at a distance for a buteo because of its size. Adults are soon recognized by their distinctive color, but young birds are far more commonly seen and suggest a young red-shouldered hawk (p. 46) or a Cooper's hawk. Cooper's shows cleaner white underparts, and the red-shouldered hawk has black wing tips and narrow white bands on its shorter tail.

In one magic day at Hawk Ridge, MN, a record 1,229 goshawks were counted.

young

goshawk

young

Goshawk

young

gyrfalcon

gray form

white form

Gyrfalcon

young

PRAIRIE AND PEREGRINE

PRAIRIE FALCON

PEREGRINE FALCON

The loud, harsh, *kik-kik-kik* territorial call of the prairie falcon is often the first clue to the bird's presence in nesting areas. Females, the larger sex, have the deeper voice.

alcons vary in size from the gyrfalcon (p. 66) to the kestrel (p. 74). Two species, the peregrine and the prairie falcon, occupy the mid-size slot (although some female peregrines are larger than some male gyrfalcons). Each finds its own niche in nature by exploiting different habitats and hunting specialties.

Prairie falcons patrol the desert and prairies of the West, where they are fairly numerous. Ground squirrels are their primary prey, but lizards and doves are important foods in some areas. In winter, horned larks, meadowlarks, and other flocking birds are their principal diet.

The prairie falcon's hunting method varies. It may spot prey from a perch, by coursing close to the ground, or from high overhead, but its final approach is almost always in swift flight close to the ground. Even when stooping from on high, the bird drops to a point some distance from the prey and closes the final yards in ground-hugging flight.

Peregrines may be found anywhere but are common nowhere. They are more interested in birds flying above a terrain than in the terrain itself. Coasts, because of their concentrations of waterbird prey, are favorite haunts. There are three distinct peregrine populations: an Arctic-nesting race, the tundra peregrine, seen in migration; a Pacific coast resident, Peale's peregrine; and an interior race, the *anatum* birds.

The interior race once nested in the East but was extirpated by DDT in the mid-1900s and now exists only in the West. Captive-bred peregrines of various races have been reintroduced in the East and elsewhere. They have adapted to bridges and buildings as well as to their original cliff nesting sites.

APLOMADO FALCON

The aplomado falcon can once again be seen in south Texas as a result of a reintroduction program begun at Laguna Atascosa **NWR** in the **1990s.**

They are about the size of prairie and peregrine falcons and were seen in southern Arizona and New Mexico as well as Texas before being extirpated in the mid-1900s.

Prairie falcons tend to bind to prey rather than clubbing it with their feet.

Peregrines typically course high in the sky. Their signature attack is a head-first stoop in which they commonly reach speeds over 100 mph. No prey out-flies them at that speed, and few animals can ignore the threat of being raked by sharp talons with such tremendous force. Peregrines sometimes bind to their prey and kill by constriction; at other times, they deliver a fatal blow with the feet.

With experience, a high-flying peregrine can be recognized by its swift, direct flight and powerful, snappy wing beat. The plumage of the different races varies, but the helmet-like sideburns are a consistent mark. Adult tundra peregrines have the least barring below and can appear nearly white, with pale gray or blue-gray upperparts. A young tundra peregrine is browner above and below and usually shows a blond crown or nape. Interior adults are dark gray to black above and are heavily

71

barred below except for a gleaming white breast. There is a cinnamon wash on the belly that extends to the breast on some birds. Young interior birds are brown streaked below. Adult Peale's are like interior birds but lack the cinnamon wash below. A young Peale's can be so dark that it resembles a young gyrfalcon.

The dark "struts" on the prairie falcon's underwings are its best marks—when they can be seen. Flying close to the ground, the "desert ghost" may appear and disappear in seconds without showing its underside. Look for brown upperparts with a pale tail. Peregrines don't show a contrast between back and tail. Prairie falcons have a moustache, but not the peregrine's broad mark or its helmeted look.

Prairie falcons are limited migrants. Only two or three dozen are recorded at Sandia, NM, and other **hawkwatches** in their range. Tundra peregrines are the ones most often seen at hawkwatches. Most migrate along the East coast. South Padre Island, TX, and Cape May, NJ, record hundreds each fall, peaking in October. Inland sites average 20 to 50 in fall.

South Padre Island also sees several hundred tundra peregrines in spring, but they fan out as they proceed north, many following the shorebirds and songbirds that migrate through the central states in spring.

prairie

peregrine

young
(soaring)

Prairie Falcon

Peregrine Falcon

tundra
form

tundra form
young

Peale's
form
young

interior form
(western)

MERLIN AND KESTREL

MERLIN

KESTREL

A merlin's attack may fail a majority of the time, but it succeeds often enough for the bird to have regular early morning and late afternoon meals.

Kestrels and merlins are small falcons with few similarities other than size. They are easily distinguished by plumage when perched and can usually be separated by shape and flight style when airborne.

Although merlins are widespread, they are common only along the Atlantic coast in fall. These birds are nearly all taiga merlins, which nest across most of Canada and Alaska. They are not as dark as the black merlins resident along the Pacific Northwest or as pale as the prairie merlins that nest in the northern Great Plains and winter primarily in the southern Great Plains. Some prairie merlins have become permanent residents in Canadian communities from British Columbia to Ontario, feeding heavily on house sparrows.

Merlins most often hunt birds and dragonflies in open areas. Beaches and tidal flats are especially popular because of the abundance of shorebirds (and, along the Atlantic coast, myrtle warblers), but prairies and marshes are also exploited. They are aggressive and swift but do not have the speed to simply overpower all smaller birds. A merlin typically attacks a flock of birds in low, direct flight. It separates a slower bird from the group and gives chase. Sometimes the chase proceeds in tight, rapidly climbing circles known as "ringing flight."

74

Kestrels are widespread and numerous in open areas as small as a vacant lot. They are perch-and-hover hunters (not power-flying predators, like other falcons) and are often seen on a utility wire eyeing the ground for a mouse or other rodent. Snakes, insects, and an occasional bird also fall prey to kestrels, which will often return daily to a fruitful perch.

Sometimes called killy hawks for their easily heard *killy, killy, killy* call, kestrels are the only hawks to nest in tree hollows. They also use small cavities in buildings and readily accept nest boxes in places with good hunting habitat.

Merlins lay their eggs in the abandoned nests of crows, hawks, or magpies.

Female kestrels are about one-quarter larger than males and much different in appearance except for the head, which is white on the cheek and throat, framed by broad black streaks. The male's detailed, colorful plumage, including blue upperwings and a brick-red tail with a wide black band, suggests an ornate military dress uniform. Females are uniformly reddish brown above, with dark barring.

Female merlins are also about one-quarter larger than males. Both sexes have similarly streaked underparts and plain faces with one vague mustache mark, but males are blue-gray above (nearly black in black merlins); females, and young birds, brown. A contrasting gray rump can sometimes be seen on adult female taiga merlins. The tail is a good mark. Tails are similar in all races and sexes, black with a narrow white tip and two to five narrow pale bands—usually two for black, three for taiga, and four for prairie merlins. Peregrines, prairie falcons, and female kestrels have more bands.

Like peregrines, kestrels and merlins migrate heaviest along the East coast, especially in fall. A good day at a coastal **hawkwatch** such as the one at Kiptopeke, VA, may mean several hundred kestrels and over 100 merlins. At Hawk Mountain, PA, or the Goshutes, NV, it takes only a few dozen kestrels and a handful of merlins to make a good day. And on the West Coast, merlins are scarce. Taiga merlins are the ones commonly seen at nearly all sites.

Fall migration runs from September through October. Spring migration extends from the end of March to early May, and inland sites see about as many birds as coastal ones—several hundred kestrels and a dozen or two merlins.

Soaring male kestrels show a distinctive line of white dots near the trailing edge of their wings that is especially obvious when backlit. The pattern can also be seen in some females.

Merlins have the direct, powerful flight typical of falcons, but kestrels fly unsteadily with fluttery wing beats. Kestrels are slender bodied and slender winged; merlins are chesty, with broad-based wings. Both often fly close to the ground. When merlins are seen soaring on a midday thermal, they show a distincive checkerboard pattern on their underwings.

76

merlin

♀　♂

kestrel

♀　♂

♀ kestrel hovering

Merlin

Kestrel

northwestern
coastal form ♀

taiga form ♀

prairie form
young

♀

taiga form
♂

♂

taiga form
♂

B oth great horned and barn owls are adaptable and may be found near civilization in lands extensively modified by man. The great horned may occupy woodlots in parks or suburbs, where it takes rodents and prey as large as skunks and other owls. It often hunts from a perch but also courses and is active at dusk and dawn as well as at night.

GREAT HORNED OWL

BARN OWL

Barn owls prefer open areas to hunt, such as fields and marshes. They typically hunt only at night and course near the ground in search of rodents, their favorite prey. Collisions with automobiles while hunting are all too common. Barn owls are famous for roosting in church steeples and barn lofts. They also occupy tree cavities and caves and use nest boxes.

Great horned owls are often recognized by their deep, rhythmic hooting: *hoo-hoo-hoo, hoo-hoo, hoo or hoo, hoo-hoo, hoo, hoo,* for instance.

The great horned owl is massive, much bulkier than the long-eared owl (p. 80), with which it may be confused. The "horns" or "ears" are farther apart on the great horned owl, which has a white throat lacking in the long-eared.

Barn owls don't hoot but give a screech or rasping hiss.

The white heart-shaped face set with dark eyes is the best mark for the barn owl. The white or cinnamon underparts and relatively long legs also contribute to its distinctive look. Barn owls are fairly numerous in their southern range but scarce and declining in the northern portion due to habitat loss from development.

Great Horned Owl

barn

Barn Owl

Although closely related, long–eared and short–eared owls live different lives. Long-eared owls are strictly nocturnal. They use concealing patches of dense woods for nesting and roosting during the day and are rarely seen. A dozen or more birds often roost together except in the nesting season. They usually perch near the trunk of a tree and often disguise themselves as upright branch stubs by stretching to become slim.

LONG-EARED OWL

SHORT-EARED OWL

Small rodents are the typical prey of both long-eared and short-eared owls. Both also migrate, and short-eared owls are occasionally noted fluttering by a hawkwatch.

Short-eared owls are scarce but more likely to be seen than long-ears because they often hunt at dusk and dawn or on overcast days. They live in open areas such as marshes and grasslands, nesting and roosting on the ground. They hunt by coursing low, slow, and buoyantly like a harrier (p. 54) but with a bouncier flight. Sometimes they hunt over the same patch of land that a harrier uses during the day.

The "ears" on the long-eared owl are usually erect and visible and distinguish it from other owls except the much bulkier and more commonly seen great horned owl (p. 78). The ears on the short-eared owl are small points that are seldom noticeable; the bird appears round-headed. In flight, short-eared and long-eared owls resemble each other, but only the short-eared is active in daylight.

Long-eared Owl

short-eared

Short-eared Owl

GREAT GRAY OWL

BARRED OWL

SPOTTED OWL

An adult male great gray averages about 2 pounds. A similar snowy owl is about 4 pounds. Females are about 40 percent heavier than males.

The apparent mass of the three owls in the genus *Strix* is largely feathers. The small yellow eyes of the great gray give a truer indication of the bird's mass than the large mask of concentric circles surrounding them. Although larger than the great horned (p. 78) or snowy owl (p. 84), it weighs less than either.

All the *Strix* owls are perch-and-drop hunters that wait patiently for prey, primarily rodents, to appear. The great gray wanders widely over cold northern and mountain forests. Its large facial discs focus sound so acutely that it hears rodents under a foot of snow and captures them sight unseen.

Barred owls (note the barring on the neck) are common in southern swamps. They also inhabit deciduous and mixed forests and are expanding into western conifers, displacing and hybridizing with spotted owls. The barred owl hoots to the cadence of *Who-cooks-for-you, who-cooks-for-you-all?*, given whole or in part.

Spotted owls are now rare in the Northwest because they hunt in the forest interior and require mature forests with an open understory for their perch-and-drop hunting style. Over 90 percent of the mature forests in the Northwest have been cut. Spotted owls have creamy spots on their heads, backs, and breasts.

Great Gray Owl

Barred Owl

Spotted Owl

HAWK OWL

SNOWY OWL

Every three to five
years snowy owls,
and to a lesser
extent hawk owls,
move farther south
in winter than usual
and in larger num-
bers. The movement
is thought to be
because of prey
scarcity in the north.
Snowy owls have
been seen as far
south as Texas.

Hawk owls and snowy owls are fairly numerous northern nomads, moving to
wherever prey is available. Both owls hunt day
or night and are bold, with little fear of hu-
mans. Snowy owls are sometimes seen in the
middle of villages or at busy airports.

Snowy owls inhabit open areas—tundra,
plains, fields, shorelines—and winter regularly
in the northern Great Plains states, less so in
New England. Lemmings are the common
prey over most of their summer range, but
snowies are not choosy. They take ptarmigan,
hares, and in winter along the shoreline, waterfowl and gulls. Adult males are the whitest,
some nearly pure white. Young birds, the
ones most often seen in the US and southern
Canada, are heavily barred with blackish
brown. Young females are the most barred.

Hawk owls typically perch conspicuously in the
top of a tree overlooking a clearing. Their pos-
ture is more horizontal than the upright stance
of other owls, and they often flick their distinctive long, rounded tails as they scan the terrain
for prey. Rodents are their summer prey
choice; grouse and other birds are winter fa-
vorites. Once prey is sighted, they swoop down
to the ground and fly swift and low to the kill.
The black borders of their facial discs and the
spotted forehead are good plumage marks.

Hawk Owl

Snowy Owl

FLAMMULATED OWL

SCREECH OWL

Eastern screech-owls give a long, mellow whinny or a long, low trill. Western screech-owls give a series of accelerating notes or a two-part trill. The whiskered screech-owls of southeastern Arizona give a series of long and short notes, like Morse code.

The red form is common only in the Southeast, and the brown form is scarce outside Florida.

Screech owls and the flammulated owl are the only small owls with ear tufts, although those on the flammulated owl are small and often flattened, so that the head appears round. Both birds are only 7 or 8 inches long, the length of a starling.

Flammulated owls are numerous but secretive. In summer they are found above 3,000 feet in western conifers and aspens, especially ponderosa pine. More often heard than seen, they give an amazingly deep-pitched, hollow *hoop,* or *hoo-hoop.* Their plumage varies from reddish to gray, from pale to dark, and from finely to coarsely mottled. Dark eyes separate them from screech owls, and red tones on the face are evident in all but the darkest gray birds. Insects are their primary prey.

Screech owls are widespread and numerous, taking a variety of small prey, including rodents, insects, and birds. They are the most likely small owl to be seen or heard in most areas. They occur in a range of colors, a score of races, and three nearly identical-looking species, which are best separated by range and calls (see sidebar). Their ear tufts can be flattened, but their facial marks and underparts are unlike those of small round-headed owls. Young birds are finely barred below rather than streaked and mottled.

Flammulated Owl

Screech Owl

red form

young

gray form

brown form

SAW-WHET OWL

BOREAL OWL

Many conservation organizations associated with Great Lakes hawkwatch sites conduct owl walks in spring or fall.

aw-whets are the most numerous and common small round-headed owl over most of the US. They are woodland birds with a preference for conifers, and they often roost low in thickets during the day, sometimes in swampy areas. Rodents are the common prey.

During migration, saw-whets accumulate at some of the same places that trap migrating hawks along the Great Lakes. Several eastern coastal sites also see good numbers. Look for them at roost in early morning after a night's migration. April is the peak time in spring; late October and early November are the fall peak.

Boreal owls are rarely encountered, and their numbers are not known. Strictly nocturnal, they roost in dense cover in northern forests and in mature conifers and aspens in western mountains. Like saw-whets, they prey primarily on rodents. In winter, boreal owls irregularly enter the northern tier of states, although the numbers and extent of the movement are not certain.

The adult boreal owl's chocolate-striped underparts distinguish it from the adult saw-whet. The black outlines on the facial disc and the pale, sometimes yellow bill are important confirming marks. Young boreal owls have distinctive dark streaks on their underparts.

Saw-whet Owl

young

young

Boreal Owl

PYGMY OWL

ELF OWL

BURROWING OWL

Ferruginous pygmy-owls are tropical owls found in parts of southern Arizona and especially in extreme south Texas. They have reddish tails with dark bars.

Pygmy owls and elf owls are tiny—simultaneously cute and fierce-looking. The burrowing owl is larger and a very different sort of owl. Colonies of burrowing owls live and nest in burrows in fields, prairies, and deserts. Prairie dog towns attract colonies, and the owls have also adapted to golf courses and airports but are declining seriously. Often one member of a pair will stand sentinel near the burrow entrance during the day. They eat insects and rodents.

Pygmy owls are a more traditional owl, albeit a tiny one. They are pugnacious little predators, taking rodents and songbirds. Songbirds hate them and mob them if found roosting during the day. They are fairly numerous in western mountain woodlands and are easy to identify by their long, banded tails. Their plumage color varies. An interesting mark is the pair of dark false eyes on the nape.

Elf owls make their homes in desert lowlands near watercourses and feed on insects and invertebrates. They use saguaros as well as trees for nesting cavities. Elf owls are nocturnal and seldom seen. They aren't often vocal either. Their small size, short tail, and indistinct breast streaks are good marks. They were once numerous throughout their range but are common now only in southern Arizona.

90

Pygmy Owl

Elf Owl

brown
extreme

gray
extreme

Burrowing Owl

young

CHECK-LIST AND INDEX

English names used in this guide and listed in the index are the familiar names used in common conversation. For the most part, they are the same as the formal English names adopted by the American Ornithologists' Union in the seventh edition of their *Check-list of North American Birds*, 1998.

When the formal AOU English name differs from the common name used in this guide, the AOU English name is given on the second line of the index entry. The Latin names in italics are the AOU's scientific names.

How many species of birds have you identified? Keeping a record is the only way to know. Sooner or later, even the most casual bird-watcher makes notes of the species seen on a trip or in a day. People keep backyard lists, year lists, state lists, every kind of list. All serious birders maintain a life list. Seeing your life list grow can become part of the pleasure of bird-watching. The pages that follow are designed to serve as your checklist of the birds of prey as well as an index to their illustrations in this guide.

Official tallies of migrating hawks at sites throughout North America are published by the Hawk Migration Association of North America. Members and volunteers of HMANA also staff many of the hawkwatches in the East and the Great Lakes and provide helpful information to all hawk-watchers, veterans and beginners alike. They maintain a site on the Internet, and copies of their publications can be obtained by writing William J. Gallagher, P.O. Box 833, Boonton, NJ, 07005-0822.

In the West, members and volunteers of HawkWatch International provide the staff for hawkwatch sites. Directions to their hawkwatches and other published information can be obtained by calling 1-800-726-4295.

✓ Species	Date	Location
◯ COMMON **B**LACK-HAWK 52 *Buteogallus anthracinus*		
◯ CRESTED **C**ARACARA 24 *Caracara plancus*		
◯ BALD **E**AGLE 28 *Haliaeetus leucocephalus*		
◯ GOLDEN **E**AGLE 28 *Aquila chrysaetos*		
◯ PEREGRINE **F**ALCON 70 *Falco peregrinus*		
◯ PRAIRIE **F**ALCON 70 *Falco mexicanus*		
◯ **G**OSHAWK 66 Northern Goshawk *Accipiter gentilis*		
◯ **G**YRFALCON 66 *Falco rusticolus*		
◯ **H**ARRIER 54 Northern Harrier *Circus cyaneus*		
◯ BROAD-WINGED **H**AWK 46 *Buteo platypterus*		
◯ COOPER'S **H**AWK 62 *Accipiter cooperii*		
◯ FERRUGINOUS **H**AWK 42 *Buteo regalis*		
◯ HARRIS' **H**AWK 52 Harris's Hawk *Parabuteo unicinctus*		
◯ RED-SHOULDERED **H**AWK 46 *Buteo lineatus*		
◯ RED-TAILED **H**AWK 32 *Buteo jamaicensis*		
◯ ROUGH-LEGGED **H**AWK 42 *Buteo lagopus*		

✓ Species	Date	Location
◯ SHARP-SHINNED HAWK 62 *Accipiter striatus*		
◯ SHORT-TAILED HAWK 50 *Buteo brachyurus*		
◯ SWAINSON'S HAWK 38 *Buteo swainsoni*		
◯ WHITE-TAILED HAWK 50 *Buteo albicaudatus*		
◯ ZONE-TAILED HAWK 52 *Buteo albonotatus*		
◯ KESTREL 74 American Kestrel *Falco sparverius*		
◯ MISSISSIPPI KITE 58 *Ictinia mississippiensis*		
◯ SWALLOW-TAILED KITE 54 *Elanoides forficatus*		
◯ WHITE-TAILED KITE 58 *Elanus leucurus*		
◯ MERLIN 74 *Falco columbarius*		
◯ OSPREY 24 *Pandion haliaetus*		
◯ BARN OWL 78 *Tyto alba*		
◯ BARRED OWL 82 *Strix varia*		
◯ BOREAL OWL 88 *Aegolius funereus*		
◯ BURROWING OWL 90 *Athene cunicularia*		
◯ ELF OWL 90 *Micrathene whitneyi*		
◯ FLAMMULATED OWL 86 *Otus flammeolus*		

✓ Species	Date	Location
◯ **GREAT GRAY OWL** *Strix nebulosa*	82	....
◯ **GREAT HORNED OWL** *Bubo virginianus*	78	....
◯ **HAWK OWL** Northern Hawk Owl *Surnia ulula*	84	....
◯ **LONG-EARED OWL** *Asio otus*	80	....
◯ **PYGMY OWL** Northern Pygmy-owl *Glaucidium gnoma*	90	....
◯ **SAW-WHET OWL** Northern Saw-whet Owl *Aegolius acadicus*	88	....
◯ **SCREECH OWL** Eastern Screech-owl *Otus asio* Western Screech-owl *Otus kennicottii* Whiskered Screech-owl *Otus trichopsis*	86	....
◯ **SHORT-EARED OWL** *Asio flammeus*	80	....
◯ **SNOWY OWL** *Nyctea scandiaca*	84	....
◯ **SPOTTED OWL** *Strix occidentalis*	82	....
◯ **BLACK VULTURE** *Coragyps atratus*	20	....
◯ **TURKEY VULTURE** *Cathartes aura*	20	....

Want to Help Conserve Birds?

It's as Easy as ABC!

By becoming a member of the American
Bird Conservancy, you can help ensure
work is being done to protect many of the
species in this field guide. You can receive *Bird
Conservation* magazine quarterly to learn about bird
conservation throughout the Americas and *World Birdwatch*
magazine for information on international bird conservation.

Make a difference to birds.
Copy this card and mail to the address listed below.

☐ **Yes,** I want to become a member and receive *Bird
Conservation* magazine.
A check in the amount of $18 is enclosed.

☐ **Yes,** I want to become an International member of
ABC and receive both *Bird Conservation* and
World Birdwatch magazines.
A check in the amount of $40 is enclosed.

NAME

ADDRESS

CITY/STATE/ZIP CODE

Return to: American Bird Conservancy
1250 24th Street NW, Suite 400; Washington, DC 20037
or call **1-888-BIRD-MAG** or e-mail: abc@abcbirds.org

Memberships are tax deductible to the extent allowable by law.